PETER LOFTUS

RECENT PAINTINGS

June 3 - July 1, 1999

HACKETT-FREEDMAN GALLERY

250 Sutter Street, 4th Floor, San Francisco, CA 94108 TEL: 415.362.7152 FAX: 415.362.7182

Cover:

Tide Pools and Ice Plant (detail)
52 x 80" oil on canvas 1999

Design: Shore Design, San Francisco
Photography: John Wilson White, Tony Grant
Coordination: Tracy Freedman, Donna Wingate
Essay © 1999, Dorothy Burkhart
All works © 1998 - 1999 Peter Loftus

CHASING THE LIGHT

DOROTHY BURKHART

Peter Loftus finds it almost impossible to explain how his luminous landscapes evolve—they surprise him as they unfold. Light-drenched pictures of the jagged cliffs, rocky shoreline, and deep woods that run along Highway 1 on California's Central Coast celebrate the magic of the light, the place, and nature. And yet, these new oils on canvas that stay rooted in reality are more complex than first meets the eye. Loftus takes every gift of the subconscious, every flash of intuition, and collaborates with what appears on the canvas. The result is a private process, an internal experience, affirming the sensual, full-bodied painting Loftus loves best.

To get to Peter Loftus' studio in Santa Cruz, you drive past breathtaking views of the coast. After climbing a broad winding street toward the University of California at Santa Cruz campus, you reach the studio. Inside it is spare and dark; Loftus is almost cut off from the beauty and light outside. But the shifting Mediterranean light that drew him to Santa Cruz from the East Coast in 1975 continues to inspire him.

Despite the immediate appeal of his subject matter, Loftus is a subtle and elusive artist, a painterly realist indebted to Impressionism, attuned to abstraction, convincingly in command of his medium. However easily he can accomplish his serene landscapes, he sets up pictorial challenges: problem-solving feeds his vision. He says, "The picture is the story and the story is about making paintings." This is not just a theory that lives outside the frame.

For these new paintings, all executed in a dazzling one-year stretch, Loftus chases the light along the coast from Pescadero to Morro Bay, until he finds a place that "showcases the look of that given day." He photographs it as a reference and frequently returns until he gets "a buzz and the place starts talking" to him.

Originally a traditional "plein-air" painter, Loftus now paints in his studio on canvases usually measuring: horizontal 52 x 80 inches; vertical 68 x 50 inches. His initial gesture is classical: a sketch on canvas, a foil with and against which to work. He blocks in major shapes, lays down dark colors—deep purple, blue violet—building up thin washes of light over dark, playing transparent against opaque, balancing all areas at once. As the composition develops, the image emerges, rendered with precision. "Basically realism is a means of channeling my improvisation and assuring a consistent focus to my impulses," Loftus says, adding that "representation allows me to paint from the heart because it gives me a fail-safe set of reference points."

Loftus has the power to act without drawing attention to the effort involved, yet energy is everywhere present in the paint. There is an element of risk in the way that he lets paint spill "on the peaks and valleys" of the canvas. Loftus is not in a hurry. The strength in the work lies in revision, second thoughts, "a cumulative thing, fields and lines that pick up and disappear, then fine-tuning," he says. Yet such moments co-habit with the improvisational quality of his method. A painterly realist who no longer seeks the splashy calligraphics of many of his contemporaries, Loftus still gets dazzling visual effects. Charting fresh territory, finding his own voice through touch and color, he fully realizes the potentials for shimmering textural richness.

Loftus' paintings are as he is. Natural, soft-spoken, direct, and confidently grounded. His paintings reflect his involvement with Zen: they are meditative. He taps into "deep non-verbal wells." He trusts in not knowing.

Through all phases of his work runs an ambitious dialogue with both past and present art. It resonates with the work of major Impressionists, Cézanne, especially Edouard Vuillard, one of his heroes from that School, as well as the distinctly American lineage of Edward Hopper, Fairfield Porter, Richard Diebenkorn, and Neil Welliver, with whom he studied at the University of Pennsylvania in Philadelphia.

But Loftus makes of Impressionism something brighter, warmer, broader. From Vuillard, Loftus gleaned compositional balance, pattern and intimacy; from Cézanne, the dynamism of push-and pull. And from Fairfield Porter, how to define an object by cutting into its bulk with strokes of the background color. Thus, in the elegant *Point Lobos Orientalesque*, background and foreground, solid and ethereal elements, seem to merge through the skillful interchange of pigments and values. Loftus' works also show reconciling contradictions between stillness and motion, close-up detail and zooming perspectives, realism and abstraction.

This is where his works invite comparison with Richard Diebenkorn, particularly the Ocean Park series. Take a painting like *Morro Bay Through Eucalyptus*, a recognizable landscape; if you turn the picture on its side, you find Diebenkorn's abstract breakup of space, his compositional scaffolding of horizontal, diagonal and vertical lines, and overlapping planes. Loftus, the great illusionist, magically takes possession of space.

With Edward Hopper and Neil Welliver, Loftus shares a realism inseparable from the presence of outdoor light, but while theirs is starkly northeastern, Loftus' is softer, hovering between airy, pale-blue and moist, hazy gray. Definitely a California painter, Loftus echoes the Coast's distinct features in atmospheric, mood-enhancing pictures that transcend subject matter, and our response becomes not merely recognition but connection to universal experience. As successfully as Loftus handles light and color, he shows equal skill in juggling composition, gambling the mass of a coastline on a spindly tree: *Rocks Near Point Lobos* and again in *Point Lobos Orientalesque*, a single frail vertical line ties foreground to deep space.

Within the California landscape genre, Loftus' distinctive paintings bridge traditional and contemporary aesthetics. He takes the genre to a renewed level of energy and expands it radiantly. Never formulaic, always unpredictable, always surprising and surprised, Loftus mesmerizes, draws us in, opening a landscape of infinite possibilities.

Dorothy Burkhart, former art critic for the *San Jose Mercury News*, is a writer, lecturer and curator working in the Bay Area. She recently curated an exhibition of Robert Cottingham's paintings.

P O I N T   L O B O S   O R I E N T A L E S Q U E
68 x 50" oil on canvas 1999

TIDE POOLS AND ICE PLANT
52 x 80" oil on canvas 1999

MORRO BAY THROUGH EUCALYPTUS

52 x 80" oil on canvas 1999

COAST NEAR CARMEL

52 x 80" oil on canvas 1998

STREAM WITH SOFT LIGHT

52 x 80" oil on canvas 1998

REFLECTIONS: PESCADERO CREEK

50 x 68" oil on canvas 1998

BOULDERS: PESCADERO CREEK

60 x 44" oil on canvas 1998

HILLS NEAR SAN SIMEON

68 x 50" oil on canvas 1999

DUSK OVER SAN GREGORIO CREEK

44 x 68" oil on canvas 1998

PETER LOFTUS

Born: 1948, Washington, DC

EDUCATION:

1974   MFA, University of Pennsylvania, Philadelphia, PA
1971   BFA, Maryland Institute College of Art, Baltimore, MD

SELECTED SOLO EXHIBITIONS:

1999   Hackett-Freedman Gallery, San Francisco, CA (also
           1997, 1996, 1992)
1998   Fischbach Gallery, New York, NY (also 1982-1997)
1994   "Close to Heart, Close to Home: Paintings of Santa
           Cruz County 1975-94", The Pope Gallery, Santa
           Cruz, CA
1991   Monterey Conference Center, Monterey, CA
1986   William Sawyer Gallery, San Francisco, CA (also 1984,
           1981, 1980)
1984   Hull Gallery, Washington, DC
1981   Redding Museum, Redding, CA
1980   San Jose Museum of Art, San Jose, CA
1979   Stevenson College, UC Santa Cruz, Santa Cruz, CA

SELECTED GROUP EXHIBITIONS SINCE 1980:

1997   "10th Anniversary Exhibition," Hackett-Freedman
           Gallery, San Francisco, CA
1996   "Contemporary American Realists," Halls Crown
           Center, Kansas City, MO (also 1994)
1995   "Realism '95: Vision and Poetry," Fletcher Gallery,
           Santa Fe, NM
           "Palette of Light," The Art Museum of Santa Cruz
           County, Santa Cruz, CA
           "Plein Air Painters," Pope Gallery, Santa Cruz, CA
           "Picture This: The Monterey Bay Region as Pictured by
           Scientists, Artists and Writers," The History Museum
           of Santa Cruz County, Santa Cruz, CA
1994   "New Bay Area Painting," Contemporary Realist
           Gallery, San Francisco, CA
1993   "Tribute," William Sawyer Gallery, San Francisco, CA
           "Contemporary Realism, Central and Northern
           California Landscapes," Monterey Peninsula Museum
           of Art, Monterey, CA
           "The Artist as Native: Reinventing Regionalism,"
           Babcock Galleries, New York, NY (traveling)
1992   "A Day in the Country, California Landscape Painting,"
           I Wolk Gallery, St. Helena, CA
1991   "New Horizons in American Realism," Flint Institute of
           Arts, Flint, MI (traveling)

1988   "The Face of the Land," Southern Alleghenies Museum
           of Art, Loretto, PA
           "The Subject is Water," Newport Art Museum,
           Newport, RI
1987-88 "Art and the Law," West Publishing Company, Eagan,
           MN (traveling)
1986   "The Painterly Landscape," Grimaldis Gallery,
           Baltimore, MD
           "Plein Air: An Exhibition of Landscape Paintings and
           Drawings," Bank of Boston, Boston, MA
1985-87 "American Realism: Twentieth Century Drawings and
           Watercolors," San Francisco Museum of Modern Art,
           San Francisco, CA (traveling)
1985   "Contemporary American Realism," Columbus Museum
           of Arts and Sciences, Columbus, GA
           "The Realist Landscape," Robeson Center Gallery,
           Rutgers University, Newark, NJ
1984   "America Seen," Adams-Middleton Gallery, Dallas, TX
1982   "Collector's Gallery XVI," Marion Koogler McNay
           Museum, San Antonio, TX

SELECTED COLLECTIONS:

American Telephone & Telegraph, New York, NY
Bank of America, San Francisco, CA
Bank of New York, New York, NY
Bechtel Corp., San Francisco, CA
Chemical Bank, New York, NY
Crocker National Bank, Midland, TX
Exxon Corp., Irving, TX
First Boston, San Francisco, CA
First International Bank, Houston, TX
Hewlett Packard, Palo Alto, CA
Hopkins, Mitchell and Carley, San Francisco, CA
Hughes Aircraft Company, Los Angeles, CA
Hughes Tool Company, Houston, TX
The Hunter Museum of Art, Chattanooga, TN
Glen C. Janss Collection, Sun Valley, ID
Merck & Company, Jersey City, New Jersey
Mitsui & Company, U.S.A., San Francisco, CA
NYNEX, New York, NY
Pacific Gas and Electric Co., San Francisco, CA
Salomon Brothers, New York, NY
San Jose Museum of Art, San Jose, CA
Saudi Royal Family, Jubail, Saudi Arabia
Southwestern Bell Corporation, Houston, TX
Wellington Management Company, Boston, MA
Wells Fargo Bank, Los Angeles, CA